Baby Farm Animals

by RONNE PELTZMAN RANDALL

illustrated by DAWN HOLMES

LADYBIRD BOOKS, INC., Auburn, Maine 04210 U.S.A.
© LADYBIRD BOOKS LTD MCMLXXXVII Loughborough, Leicestershire, England

Printed in U.S.A.

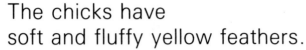
The chicks have
soft and fluffy yellow feathers.

These woolly lambs are
out in the meadow, ready to play.

These lambs have come into the barn for a snack.

Baby donkey goes for a run
while her brother waits under a tree.

These ducklings
like their comfortable nest
in the farmyard.

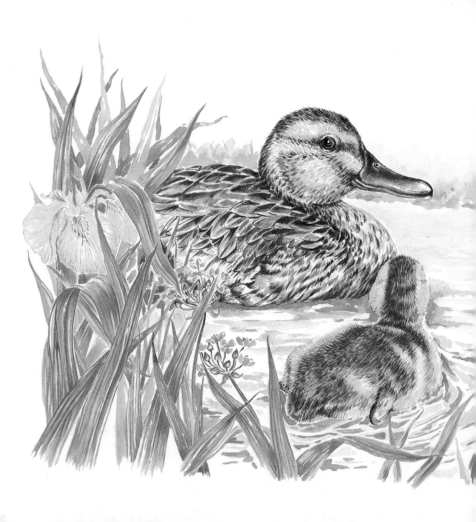

These ducklings
are out for a swim with their mother.

The calves like to chew
the sweet green grass.

There is lots of hay in the barn for these calves to eat.

The long-legged foal
has a white patch
on her face.

The baby goat watches
his sister walk through the flowers.
Will he follow her?

The plump pink piglets
stay close to their mother.

The baby geese nestle together
in the tall grass.